SECOND ANNUAL CONFERENCE

OF THE

YOUNG PEOPLE'S SOCIETIES

OF

CHRISTIAN ENDEAVOR CONVENTION

HELD AT

Payson Memorial Church, Portland,

Me.,

June 7th, 1883.

With Papers at the Conference.

First Fruits Press
Wilmore, Kentucky
c2015

First Fruits Press
The Academic Open Press of Asbury Theological Seminary
204 N. Lexington Ave., Wilmore, KY 40390
859-858-2236
first.fruits@asburyseminary.edu
asbury.to/firstfruits

SECOND ANNUAL CONFERENCE

—OF THE—

Young People's Societies

—OF—

CHRISTIAN ENDEAVOR,

HELD AT THE

PAYSON MEMORIAL CHURCH,

PORTLAND, ME.,

JUNE 7th, 1883:

WITH PAPERS READ ON THE OCCASION.

BURLINGTON:
R. S. STYLES, STEAM BOOK AND JOB PRINTER,
1883

INTRODUCTORY NOTE.

As all those into whose hands this pamphlet may fall may not be acquainted with the Society of Christian Endeavor, a few words concerning its history and aims will not be inappropriate. The first Young People's Society of Christian Endeavor was organized February, 1881, in Williston Congregational Church, Portland, Maine.

During the preceding weeks a gracious revival had blessed the young people, in connection with Sunday School prayer meetings which had been held directly after the session of the Sunday School, and a large number had become hopeful Christians. Many of these young Christians were boys and girls from ten to fifteen years of age.

The practical questions which have frequently troubled pastors at once arose : What shall be done for these young Christians? How shall they be set to work ? How shall they be kept near to Him whom, with faltering steps, they have begun to follow ? Is it safe to admit them all to the church at once ? How shall the gap between conversion and church membership,—often a long gap with young children,—be safely bridged over?

With these unsolved practical questions pressing upon his heart the pastor of the Williston Church invited the young people to his house one evening and there proposed to them that they band themselves together in a voluntary association for Christian effort. A constitution, which was substantially the one now adopted by most Societies, was read and accepted, and the first Young People's Society of Christian Endeavor was established, amid many trembling hopes and fears.

It succeeded beyond the expectations of its founders ; the young people were faithful to their vows, enthusiastic in the support of their meetings, far more devoted than ever before to the interests of the church, and willing to be guided by the larger experience of pastor and older friends, while the Society rendered the practical oversight and guardianship of the Young Christians possible and easy. The success of this plan gradually became known to others who were looking in this same direction of Christian Nurture, and was tried in other places. Wherever sufficient pains were taken and hard work was put into it by young-hearted, older Christians, it succeeded admirably; languishing young people's prayer meetings revived; latent Christian activity was brought out; faith in youthful piety was increased in the churches; child church membership became expedient and desirable where formerly it had been looked upon as a doubtful experiment, and many churches reported large accessions to their ranks and a great increase of religious interest.

In June, 1882, a conference of Societies of Christian Endeavor was held in the Williston Church, Portland, at which reports were presented which showed the efficacy of the organization, and a new impetus was given to the work.

In January, 1883, a book was published upon the subject of Christian Nurture styled "The Children and the Church," detailing the aims and methods of this Society, and this book has already had a large sale.

In June, 1883, the second annual conference was held in the Payson Memorial Church, of which this pamphlet contains the report. It is well that the cardinal principles of the Society should be fully understood. It starts on the principle that a child, through the influence of the Spirit of God, may become a christian very early. It proceeds upon the principle that he needs special watchfulness, care and training to make him strong and serviceable in the household of God. Account for it as we may, there has been a sad lack in the home training and the church training of young Christians. The lack has not been so much in the line of instruction as in the line of practice, and earnest Christian effort suited to a youth's or child's experience and capacities.

The Society of Christian Endeavor aims to accomplish for the *training* of the youthful convert in the Christian life what the Sunday accomplishes for his *instruction* in the Christian life.

Instruction and training must necessarily go together, to a large extent; but while the Sunday School *emphasizes* the one, the Society *emphasizes* the other. In bringing about this end the Society lays great stress upon frequent confession of love to Christ, requires some part to be taken by all the members, in all the meetings, and sets apart one evening each month for the renewal of vows of allegiance to the Master, at what is called the experience meeting. Besides this, effort in the line of benevolence, care of the sick, help for the Sunday School, Christian watch and care one of another, and innumerable methods of humble Christ-like activity may be introduced. But we need not enlarge upon these points, as a study of the constitution here printed will give a fair idea of the work the Society undertakes.

One point more. Let it always be understood that the Society is simply and only a humble helpmeet of the church. It works in the church, and through the church, and for the church. In no instance has it been known to distract from the church the interest of the young people, or to monopolize their efforts to the detriment of the church. In many instances has it been known to quicken the interest of the young in the church and of the church in the young. Until the church has been ready to receive the children, the Society has often kept them from lapsing into a state of carelessness and indifference, from which state a second awakening is most difficult.

The Young People's Society of Christian Endeavor has been called a Half-Way House to the church, a Training School in the church, and a Watch Tower for the church. All this it aims to be, and is, whenever sufficient, self-denying, wisely directed labor is spent upon it.

The practical papers here presented in this report of the Conference of 1883 are by those who have been actually engaged in the work, and who know whereof they affirm. They, every one, speak the results of experience, and are answers to innumerable questions which are constantly arising. The Secretary's report shows the growth and present prospects of the organization, though it is necessarily incomplete, as but a small fraction of the Societies reported in season for the Conference.

This pamphlet is sent out in the hope that it may obtain the careful attention of those who receive it, and that it may have some humble part in solving the great and increasingly difficult problem of Christian Nurture.

We append the Constitution adopted by many of the Societies that all may understand the principles of the organization:

F. E. C.

CONSTITUTION OF THE WILLISTON YOUNG PEOPLE'S SOCIETY OF CHRISTIAN ENDEAVOR.

Name. This Society shall be called the "Williston Young People's Society of Christian Endeavor."

Object. Its object shall be to promote an earnest Christian life among its members, to increase their mutual acquaintance, and to make them more useful in the service of God.

Membership. The members shall consist of two classes, Active and Associate.

Active Members.—The Active Members of this Society shall consist of all young people who sincerely desire to accomplish the results above specified. They shall become members upon being elected by the Society, and upon signing their names to the book, thereby agreeing to live up to the requirements of the constitution.

Associate Members.—Any young person who is not at present willing to be considered a decided Christian, may join this Society as an Associate Member. Such a one shall have the privileges of the Society, and shall have the special prayers and sympathy of the active members, but shall be excused from taking part in the prayer-meetings. It is hoped and expected that all associate members will in time become active members, and the Society will work and pray for this end.

The Lookout Committee shall, by personal interview, satisfy themselves of the fitness of young persons to become members of this Society, and shall propose their names at least one week before their election by the Society.

Officers. The officers of this Society shall be a President, Vice President and Secretary, whose duties shall be those which usually fall to such officers.

There shall also be a Prayer-meeting Committee, a Lookout Committee, a Social Committee, a Missionary Committee, a Sunday School Committee, and a Flower Committee, each consisting of five members.

The Prayer-meeting Committee. This Committee shall have in charge the Friday evening prayer-meeting, shall see that a topic is assigned, and a leader provided for each meeting.

The Lookout Committee. It shall be the duty of the Lookout Committee to bring new members into the Society, to introduce them into the work, and to the other members, and to affectionately look after and reclaim any that seem to be indifferent to their duties.

The Social Committee. It shall be the duty of the Social Committee to provide for the mutual acquaintance of the members by occasional sociables, for which any entertainment that may be desired may be provided.

The Missionary Committee. It shall be the duty of the Missionary Committee to raise money for benevolent objects by voluntary contributions or by entertainments, to distribute the same according to their best judgment, and to account for all money thus raised to the Society. A sum not exceeding one-fourth of all the money thus raised may, if deemed necessary, be used for the current expenses of the Society. It shall be the duty of this Committee also to provide for an occasional missionary meeting, and to interest the members of the Society in all ways in missionary topics.

The Sunday School Committee. It shall be the duty of this Committee to seek out cases of sickness and suffering among the members of the Society, to bring them to the notice of the other members, and, so far as possible, to relieve those who may be in want.

The Flower Committee. It shall be the duty of this Committee to provide flowers for the pulpit on Sunday, whenever practicable, and afterward to distribute the same to the sick, whenever it may be possible to do so.

Reports of Committees. Each Committee shall make a report to the Society at the monthly business meeting, concerning the work of the past month.

Business Meetings and Elections. Business meetings can be held at the close of the Friday evening meeting, or at any other time, in accordance with the call of the President. An election of officers and committees shall be held once in six months. Names may be proposed by a Nominating Committee appointed by the President.

The Prayer Meeting. It is expected that all the active members of this Society will be present at every meeting, unless detained by some absolute necessity, and that each one will take some part, however slight, in every meeting. The meetings shall be held just one hour, and at the close, some time may be taken for introduction and social intercourse, if desired. *Once each month, an experience meeting shall be held, at which each member shall speak concerning his progress in the Christian life for the past month.* If any one chooses, he can express his feelings by an appropriate verse of scripture. *It is expected that if any one is obliged to be absent from this experience meeting he will send the reason for such absence by some one who attends.*

At the close of the monthly experience meeting, the roll shall be called, and the response of the active members who are present shall be considered a renewed expression of allegiance to Christ; and if any member of the Society is absent from the monthly experience meeting, and fails to send an excuse, the Lookout Committee is expected to take the name of such an one, and, in a kindly and brotherly spirit, ascertain the reason of the absence. *If any member of this Society is absent and unexcused from three consecutive experience meetings, such an one ceases to be a member of the Society, and his name shall be stricken from the list of members.*

Miscellaneous. Any other committees may be added and duties assumed by this Society which may in the future seem best.

This constitution can be amended by a two-thirds vote of the Society, provided that notice of such amendment is given in writing, and recorded by the Secretary, at least one week before the amendment is acted upon.

MINUTES.

The Second Annual Conference of the Societies of Christian Endeavor was called to order by the President, W. H. Pennell, Esq., in the Vestry of the Second Parish Church, at 10 o'clock, Thursday morning, June 7.

In accordance with a motion to that effect, the Chair appointed the following Committees:

On Credentials—Bros. J. W. Stevenson, Harris M. Barnes, C. H. Oldham.

On Business—Bros. F. Brunell, F. W. Hall, W. H. Wood.

On Nominations—Rev. S. W. Adriance, Bros. G. Staples, C. H. Oldham.

On Finance—Bros. A. B. Hall, H. H. Burgess, Wm. J. Van Patten.

On Question Box—Rev. F. E. Clark, Rev. S. W. Adriance, Rev. G. H. Lockwood.

Social Committee—Rev. F. E. Clark, Bros. Granville Staples, M. E. Shedd, Fred Brunell and Miss Anna Garland.

The following Societies were found to be represented by the following delegates:

Portland, Me. (Williston). Rev. F. E. Clark, W. H. Pennell, H. B. Pennell, Miss Nellie N. Jordan, Miss Anna M. Garland, Miss Hattie A. Jordan, Harris M. Barnes, Clarence A. Hight.

Portland, (Second Parish). J. W. Stevenson, Mrs. Adams, Mrs. Hutchinson, Miss Mabel Leach, W. D. Caruthers, Fred W. Fogg.

Portland, (West Church). Rev. J. C. Holbrook, D. D., Chas. S. Palmer, Charles Bolton, F. C. Blake.

Portland, (First Baptist). Rev. A. K. P. Small, D. D., A. B. Hall, C. H. Oldham, Mrs. C. H. Oldham, Fred Brunell, Miss Helen S. Robinson.

Portland, (Casco St. Free Baptist Church). Rev. J. M. Lowden, Oliver B. T. Wish.

Portland, (St. Lawrence St.) H. H. Burgess, Geo. L. Gerish,

Granville Staples, Benj. Thompson, Mrs. Benj. Thompson, A. Munnish.

Woodfords, Me. Rev. S. W. Adriance, Mrs. S. W. Adriance, F. V. Matthews, H. C. Haskell, Miss Georgie M. Blackstone, Miss Carrie A. Bailey, A. F. Hill.

Kennebunk, Me. Rev. G. A. Lockwood, H. S. Brigham, Mrs. H. S. Brigham, Mrs. E. H. Beckford.

Cumberland Centre, Me. P. M. Leighton, Mrs. Lizzie Rideout, Miss Carrie Watson.

Bucksport, Me. Mrs. A. F. Page, Miss Gardiner, Miss Lincoln.

Biddeford, Me. Rev. E. C. Andrews, Miss Hattie Staples, Miss Sadie Littlefield.

Freeport, Me. Rev. P. B. Wing, W. S. Aldrich, Miss Clara Pettingill, Frank E. Merrill.

Limington, Me. Rev. E. T. Pitts, Miss Ella Boothby, Miss Inez Lord.

Norway, Me. Rev. A. Wiswall.

Burlington. Vt. (First Cong'l Church). W. J. Van Patten, M. E. Shedd, W. H. Wood, Miss Emma Rice, Miss May Lemon.

Lowell, Mass. (Kirk St. Church). Samuel Sewall, Frank W. Hall.

Boston, Mass. (Immanuel Church). Royal T. G. Brown.

Great Falls, N. H. H. A. Buffum, Miss Mattie T. Walker.

Milton, N. H. Rev. George Sterling.

At 10.30 an interesting devotional meeting was conducted by Rev. J. M. Lowden, pastor of the Free Baptist Church, Portland.

At 11 o'clock the subject, "The Work of the Social Committee" was opened by Mr. Granville Staples of the St. Lawrence Street Church, Portland, Me.

At 11.30 "The relation of the Society to the Church" was opened by a paper by Rev. F. E. Clark, pastor of the Williston Church, Portland.

This discussion was participated in by Bros. Van Patten, of Burlington, Vermont, Brown of Boston, Hill of Woodfords, Stevenson of Portland, and by Rev. Messrs. Sterling of Milton, N. H., and Lowden of Portland.

The main point insisted on by all the speakers was that the Society should in no case be allowed to usurp the place of the church in the minds of the young people. The church must always be first, and its meetings considered of prime importance. The universal testimony was that the Society had increased the attendance and usefulness of young people in the regular church meetings.

At 12 o'clock the following question was opened by Mr. J. W. Stevenson of Second Parish Church, Portland, Secretary of the Conference : "The Experience Meetings—how to conduct them."

Rev. S. W. Adriance said : "In our Society at the experience meeting the roll is called at the beginning. Each one responds by a verse of scripture, or in their own words, as their names are called. When a half dozen names or so have been called there is a hymn sung, followed by a prayer; after which we go on with the roll call as before, and so the whole hour is spent." The question was further discussed by Bros. Staples, Pennell of Portland, Hall of Lowell, and Rev. Messrs. Lowden and Clark of Portland, and the idea was made prominent that the Experience Meetings should be for *reconsecration, recommitment* to Christ, in some simple way. The name "Experience Meeting" is sometimes misleading, as only the simplest testimony of love to Christ should be *demanded* from each one.

Conference adjourned until 2 P. M.

Afternoon Session.

Two o'clock P. M.

After devotional exercises the Committee on Finance submitted the following report, which was accepted and adopted:

> Your Committee on Finance would report that it seems to be wise to provide for printing quite a large number of reports of this Conference, for distribution. To provide means for that, we recommend that the Societies here represented pledge themselves to contribute a sum not less than one hundred dollars, and that a contribution be asked at this evening's service.
>
> A. B. HALL,
> H. H. BURGESS,
> W. J. VAN PATTEN,
> Committee.

The Committee on Credentials reported through their chairman, Mr. J. W. Stevenson. The report was accepted and adopted.

The Committee on Nominations reported through its chairman, Rev. S. W. Adriance.

Voted to accept their report and proceed to the election of officers by acclamation. The following officers of the Conference, for the ensuing year, were unanimously elected:

President—W. H. Pennell, Portland, Me.

Vice Presidents—Maine, Rev. F. E. Clark, Portland; Vermont, Rev. L. O. Brastow, Burlington; Massachusetts, Rev. C. A. Dickinson, Lowell; New York, Rev. Theodore W. Hopkins, Rochester; New Jersey, Rev. R. W. Brokaw, Belleville; Wisconsin, C. A. Stone, Racine; Minnesota, Rev. E. L. Morse, Glyndon; Iowa, Rev. C. A. Towle, Monticello; Illinois, Rev. L. L. Kneeland, Kankakee; Missouri, Rev. C. L. Goodell, D. D., St. Louis; California, Rev. J. K. McLean, D. D., Oakland.

Secretary—J. W. Stevenson, Esq., Portland, Me.

Treasurer—W. J. Van Patten, Esq., Burlington, Vt.

Executive Committee—Rev. F. E. Clark, Rev. J. M. Lowden, Rev. C. A. Dickinson, H. H. Burgess, Esq., W. H. Pennell, Esq.

At 2.30 the following question was opened by Bro. W. J. Van Patten of Burlington, Vt., "Ways and Means of Extending the Work."

In the discussion which followed by Rev. Messrs. Wing of Freeport, Lockwood of Kennebunk, Clark of Portland, and Adriance of Woodford, and by Bros. Shedd and Wood of Burlington, Barnes, Pennell and Staples of Portland, and Page of Bucksport, the importance of thorough organization was insisted on; the holding of County Conferences was recommended, and the desirability of pastors and others informing the public through the papers of the workings of the Society was urged.

At 3 o'clock the question "The Relation of the Society to the Sunday School" was opened by H. H. Burgess, Esq., of the St. Lawrence Street Society, Portland. The discussion was continued by Revs. C. E. Andrews, G. A. Lockwood and P. B. Wing, and Bros. Wood, Shedd, Barnes, Pennell, Gage, and Staples. It was suggested that in the Sabbath School the seed was sown, while in the young people's meetings it had achance to grow.

It was felt by many that Union Societies among different denominations were not wise; that each Society should be a feeder to some particular church, as each Sunday School is. The helpful work of a Sunday School Committee was alluded to.

At 3.30 the question "Who may become Members" was opened by Rev. S. W. Adriance of Woodfords.

Discussion of the question followed by Bros. Sewall of Lowell, Gilman, Pennell and Brunell of Portland, and Rev. Mr. Wing of Freeport. All who are young hearted and who sympathize cordially with the young in their efforts to grow in grace should be admitted. No strict age line on either side can be drawn.

At 4 o'clock the following question "Our Rules; how strictly should they be enforced?" was opened by the President of the Conference, W. H. Pennell, Esq., of Portland.

Bros. Brown, Staples, Brunell, Van Patten, Oldham, Sewall and Page participated in this discussion. The general idea advanced was that a strict interpretation of the rules should be insisted on, especially the prayer-meeting rules, as vital to the prosperity of the Society. This is the distinctive rule of the organization, and must be insisted on.

At 4.30 came the question "How may young ladies assist in

this work?" Opened by Miss Ada Sewall, of the Second Parish Church, Portland.

Miss Garland, from the beginning chairman of the Lookout Committee of the Williston Society, emphasized the opportunity which young ladies have of helping the work by social calls at the homes of the young people.

Rev. Mr. Wiswall of Norway, and Rev. Dr. Holbrook of Portland spoke of the great assistance which young ladies may afford, and the great opportunity here given them to work.

At 6 o'clock the last question for the afternoon was opened by Bro. E. L. Sayward of the Williston Society, "How does the Society help young Christians?" This address was not written, and we regret to say was not reported. The various ways in which the organization was helpful to young Christians, as seen by a young Christian, were ably set forth. Bro. Wood of Burlington liked the name "Christian *Endeavor*." The very name showed how the Society helps young Christians. Bro. Haskell of Woodfords, one of the youngest members present, said the first time he spoke he couldn't think of anything to say, so he said just what the one before him had said, but experience had given him more confidence and strength, so that now he was always glad to declare his love for the Master, and thus the meetings had helped him.

A paper, prepared by Bro. Frank W. Hall, of the Kirk Street Society, Lowell, Mass., conveying the greeting of his Society, and rehearsing the way in which it was established, was, through inadvertance, not presented to the Conference. It will be found, however, in plaee, and it is hoped that it will show the initial stages of such an organization, how it may be started, and become a power in the church.

Adjourned to 7.30 P. M.

Evening Session.

At 7.30 the exercises were opened by a half-hour praise meeting conducted by Bro. A. B. Hall of the First Baptist Church. The singing was very spirited, and the meeting much enjoyed.

The report of the Secretary, Bro. J. W. Stevenson, was then read.

The following pledges were then made for the expenses incurred in printing the Minutes, &c. :

Second Parish, Portland,	$5.00
Kirk Street, Lowell, Mass.,	10.00
Woodfords, Maine,	5.00
Burlington, Vermont,	10.00
First Baptist, Portland,	10.00
Williston, Portland,	10.00
Free Baptist, Portland,	5.00
St. Lawrence Street, Portland,	5 00
Immanuel Church, Boston,	5.00
Freeport, Maine,	5.00
West Church, Portland,	3.00

Mr. Samuel Sewall, of Kirk Street Church, Lowell, gave the Conference a hearty invitation to meet with their Society next year, which was cordially accepted.

On motion, it was voted to leave the time of the next meeting to the Executive Committee, in conference with the Society in Lowell.

The Question Box exercise was then conducted by Rev. F. E. Clark of Portland. More than thirty questions had been handed in, many of them of great interest. They were ably answered by members from the floor.

A vote was then passed expressing the thanks of the Conference to the Second Parish Church for the use of their beautiful church, and to the Society of Christian Endeavor in the Second Parish Church for their bountiful hospitality.

A fine collation was provided for the visitors by the young ladies, both at dinner and supper time, and everything possible was done for the comfort of the guests.

After a brief closing address by the President, Mr. W. H. Pennell, prayer was offered by Rev. A. K. P. Small, D. D., of the First Baptist Church, Portland; the hymn "Blest be the tie that binds" was sung, and the Benediction was pronounced by Dr. Small.

Conference adjourned *sine die*.

PAPERS ON PRACTICAL TOPICS CONNECTED WITH THE WORK OF THE YOUNG PEOPLE'S SOCIETIES OF CHRISTIAN ENDEAVOR,

Read at the Second Annual Conference, Portland, June 7, 1883.

THE WORK OF THE SOCIAL COMMITTEE. Mr. Granville Staples, Portland.

THE RELATION OF THE SOCIETY TO THE CHURCH. Rev. F. E. Clark, Portland.

THE EXPERIENCE MEETINGS. Mr. J. W. Stevenson, Portland.

WAYS AND MEANS OF EXTENDING THE WORK. Mr. W. J. Van Patten, Burlington, Vt.

THE RELATION OF THE SOCIETY TO THE SUNDAY SCHOOL. Mr. H. H. Burgess, Portland.

WHO MAY BECOME MEMBERS? Rev. S. W. Adriance, Woodford.

OUR RULES. Mr. W. H. Pennell, Portland.

HOW MAY YOUNG LADIES ASSIST IN THE WORK? Miss Ada Sewall, Portland.

PRACTICAL EXPERIENCE IN ESTABLISHING A SOCIETY. Mr. F. W. Hall, Lowell, Mass.

SECRETARY'S REPORT. Mr. J. W. Stevenson, Portland.

THE WORK OF THE SOCIAL COMMITTEE.

By Mr. Granville Staples,
Of the St. Lawrence Street Society, Portland, Maine.

Put the best persons on this committee, not anyone that happens to be able to make sport. Some think that anyone will do for this work. This is a mistake. We want people who can enter into a good time with the youngest, and enjoy it, and yet we want those who are thorough Christians, so that even in their games they will influence all for Christ.

I know a man who was pastor of one of the churches of this State but now has gone to another field of labor, whom I think I shall always hold in great respect because of his ability to play croquet, and to play it like a Christian, so all could see that he was a Christian. Now, for the work of this Committee I should say,—

1st. Pray. I do not know that all will think that our amusements are things to pray about, but it seems to me that the Social Committee should be a praying committee, praying about their games, praying that the sociable shall be the means of bringing each member near to Jesus, praying that it may make us love each other better as brothers and sisters, as friends and companions.

2d. Make a plan for the sociables. Don't let it happen as it may; and yet don't be too rigid with your plan. If, after you have your plan, there is a better way found, be glad to go in for that.

Have a plan so that when things come to a stand-still, as they will, at times, you will not be at your wit's end to know what to do next.

3d. Be sure and have some wide-awake games at each sociable. Music is good; but, remember boys and girls were not made to sit still and listen to you for two hours; remember that their hands and tongue all ache to go.

Some of us used to know what it was to find ourselves in a company where all were talking except a few boys and girls who stood for the whole evening in one spot against the wall, wishing that we were at home. Don't let the boys feel that way; start them going, and they will be all right for the rest of the evening.

4th. Have a leader, who is able to hold the reins, and guide the whole sociable in the right way. Boys and girls will get unruly if left to themselves, so have some one that they love and respect to be the leader.

5th. Look out for the wall-flowers. See that every one is having a good time. If games are being played, be sure and play yourselves, and keep your eyes open to see if any one is slighted. Some girls will be selected twice as often as others—look out for the others.

One young friend of mine was brought to Christ, so he thinks, by being noticed by two ladies, where he was a stranger, in one of our church sociables.

6th. Don't let any of the older members sit back when the games for the younger ones are being played, thinking they are too old to engage in such games. It has a bad effect. It will do the older ones good to play Blindman's Buff, fox and geese, etc. It will take the stiffness out of their joints. It will not hurt the pastor or deacon's coat-tails to be seen waving in the air as they are on the chase with some of the younger ones : that is, if they are true men, and do not have to put on long faces, so that people will know that they are deacons.

7th. Keep good hours. A great many parents do not like to have their children out late evenings, and that is where they are right. So do not hold the sociable later than 9 or at the latest 9½ o'clock.

8th. Let it be understood that the sociables are for the members of the Society only, and not for all. Our constitution says that "It shall be the work of the Social Committee to provide for the mutual acquaintance of *members* by occasional sociables."

THE RELATION OF THE YOUNG PEOPLE'S SOCIETY OF CHRISTIAN ENDEAVOR TO THE CHURCH.

By Rev. F. E. Clark,

Pastor of the Williston Church, Portland, Maine.

This question is as important as it is practical. There are two dangers to be guarded aganst : first, that the church shall regard such an organization of young people with distrust, and shall withhold from them the sympathy and encouragement which they need ; and, second, that the young people shall consider their society an end in itself, without reference to the church, and shall endeavor to set up a second church, a young people's church, and thus widen the breach between old and young.

These dangers have frequently been enlarged upon and much exaggerated, we think. However, they are real dangers, and it is well that we give heed to them, when we consider the relations of the Society to the church. "We are afraid of this Society plan," says the N. Y. *Independent.* "The surest way of ruining a church and of taking all of its life and usefulness out of it is to remove from its agency just such department of work as this. Such a plan is a sort of plundering of the church of the most profitable parts of its business."

Such ill-considered criticism sounds quite absurd in view of what has actually been accomplished, and the strength instead of weakness which has come to many a church through these very Societies ; but it is always well to learn, even from our enemies, and we learn from this piece of hostile criticism, which is almost the only one that I have observed, the point which we need especially to guard, and that is to keep the relation of these societies to the church a close and intimate one. This intimate feeling of relationship should be encouraged in every way. All expressions or sentiments which seem to imply that there is any division of interest between the Society and the church should be frowned upon and discouraged. If the older christians complain that there is a lack of interest in the church shown by the younger members, they should take special pains to disprove this charge by actions which manifest interest in and solicitude for the church.

Let all the young people get into the habit of thinking and speaking of "*our* church," and "*our* prayer-meetings," and "*our* minister," as well as of "*our* Society." There is a great deal of difference between "*our*" and "*your*." Be sure and use the right pronoun when speaking of the church with which you are connected.

One Young People's Society of Christian Endeavor, in Massachusetts, is called "The Church Porch," a good name, so far as it signifies the intimate relationship between the Society and the church. As close as the porch is to the house, so close should be the Society to the church.

Again, the relationship should be not only an intimate one, but a dependent one. The young people should feel that their Society *is* the *porch* and not the *church*. The church is the main institution. It is established by God, and is the only organization thus established. All other agencies for the conversion of the world and for the growth in grace of Christians,—the Sunday School, the Church Prayer-Meeting, the Young Men's Christian Associations, as well as our Young People's Societies,—are secondary, and should be dependent on the church for their life and growth. They should be in the bosom of the church, working for the church and through the church.

It follows, in the third place, that if this relationship of the Young People's Societies to the church is intimate and dependent, that its attitude should be deferential. The wishes of the older (and presumably wiser) church members should be deferred to, so far as possible. There should be no arrogance or uppishness on the part of the young people. In any case of conflict of opinion the matter should be looked at calmly by the young people, who should remember that their interests are entirely one with the interests of the church, that what is good for the church is good for the Society, and they should try, as far as they can, to look at any such matters through the spectacles of older Christians.

Once more, the relation of the Young People's Societies to the church should be not only *intimate, dependent* and *deferential*, but in every way *helpful*. The young people, especially those who belong to the church, should endeavor to be at the church prayer-meetings as well as at their own. Whenever any workmen are needed, they should volunteer. Their voices should be heard in prayer or remark, sometimes, in the regular prayer-meetings as well as in their own. The pastor and officers of the church should feel that they can count on the young Christians whoever else they cannot count on. Are there circulars to be distributed, errands to be done, collections to be made, subscription papers to be passed, parlor entertainments to be provided, the young Christians of the Societies of Christian Endeavor should hold themselves ready for all these emergencies.

In the early days of our revolutionary war, before the army was thoroughly organized, what were called minute-men were scattered throughout New England; men ready at a moment's notice to leave the plow and catch up the musket and fight for their country. Every member of our Young People's Societies should be a minute-man, ready at a moment's notice to do any work that may be required of them.

One Society in Boston I hear has chosen for its local name, "The Pastor's Aid Society,"—a good name again, so far as it expresses the helpful side of these organizations. Says Dr. Goodell, of his Society in St. Louis: "It is one of the special helps to the pastor. It is wings for him, and flies all over the city." Let this be true of every Society of Christian Endeavor.

One very stormy evening a few weeks ago, when the wind howled and the rain fell in torrents, there were only thirty-five people present at our weekly church prayer-meeting at Williston Church, and among these I counted twenty-three young people, who belong to the Society of Christian Endeavor, and who always sustain the Friday evening meeting. Such a record I think shows the helpful relationship of the Society to the church.

To turn for a moment to the other side. What should be the relation of the Church to the Society?

I know of no better word to use than the one just used to express the other side of the relationship,—it should be *helpful*. If the Society should be helpful to the church, the church surely should be helpful to the Society. It should not be fussy, critical, fault-finding. It should remember that while the boys and girls are christians, they are boys and girls still, and it should endeavor to throw around them all, arms of love and sympathy. It should treat them as parents treat the children in their own home, making excuses for immaturity and lack of judgment, encouraging well-meant effort, and always speaking a kind word for the boys and girls among outsiders, who are inclined to view them critically. Above all, the carping, fretting spirit should be detested. If criticisms are to be made they should be made privately and kindly and in a way to lead the young Christians to believe that the older ones have a real interest in and love for them.

Now comes the question, perhaps, should the church choose the officers of the Society, as it frequently does in the Sunday School? I think not. The young people should be trusted to do this for themselves, and they will probably be better satisfied with officers of their own choice. If the pastor and a few more mature Christians are interested and active in this work, there is little danger, we think, that the young people will go far astray.

Again, it may be asked to what extent should the older Christians attend and take part in these meetings? This must be, largely, not a matter of rule but of evident adaptability. Every one is or should be aware of their own limitations, and many, perhaps most older christians, know that they can best aid their younger brethren and sisters not by coming to and taking part in all their meetings, but by encouraging them by a friendly attitude, and by speaking kind words to them and of them, outside of their meeting.

A *few* in every church will, doubtless, feel their adaptability to this work, and can be especially useful just here, even if they have seen more than two score years and ten. Here, then, is the place for them. Never, however, should the older members take up so much time in the meetings that the younger will feel that they are cut off from their opportunities or absolved from their obligations. We should put a special guard upon ourselves at this point and be very brief in our remarks at every young people's meeting, putting the burden and responsibility upon them. But it is not necessary to dwell longer upon these obvious relations of the older church members and the Society. To sum up in one phrase : If the relation of the Society to the church should be intimate, dependent, deferential, helpful, the relation of the church to the Society should be kindly, charitable, uncritical, in a word—motherly.

If the Church is the mother of us all, let her regard the Young People's Society of Christian Endeavor as her elder daughter, who will aid her, and whom she will aid in training the younger children of the church.

Then let the elder daughter give honor, respect, love and hearty helpfulness to her venerable mother, let the mother give confidence and cordial support to her elder daughter, all for the training of the boys and girls in Christ's own ways of peace and righteousness.

THE EXPERIENCE MEETINGS—HOW TO CONDUCT THEM.

By Mr. J. W. Stevenson.

Christian life and Christian experience are inseparable. Nay ! are they not almost synonymous terms ? How important, then, is the subject we are about to discuss ! How reverently we should come to it ! Do we find some Christian lives stunted, gnarled, almost fruitless ? Yes, too many ! But they ought not to be, they need not be ! They need not be ? But how prevent it, how reclaim them ? By drawing out and developing the Christian experience. It becomes then a practical question—How can we develop a Christian experience ?

From the very nature of experience it is manifest that self-surrender, or consecration, is the first step. Experience is the result of personal contact, but it is not experience unless the contact makes an impression. If the hand is completely benumbed and it is thrust into a fire there is no pain experienced, not because there is no contact, but because there is no impression; and so, unless we give up our own wills and submit ourselves wholly to God, we are not in that impressible state that will make an experience possible. And so, in the first place, to make an experience possible we must consecrate ourselves. Do we sometimes wonder why our experiences are not as clear and distinct as we desire to have them ? May we not find the answer in the fact that there has not been a complete self-surrender ?

It is to be feared that too many are satisfied with the passive condition of receiving the impressions of experience and forget that they are sent for a purpose, and this leads us to a second and important point in the development of our experiences.

We must not allow our experiences to be like the sparkling dew drops which flash back the bright rays of the morning sun, but which soon are lost to sight in vapor; while the leaves on which they have rested become dry and withered.

Unless our experiences are retained to give freshness and vigor for the hours of toil and trial we shall find that the fierce fires of evil will shrivel and wilt us as the hot sun does the dew covered leaves when the dew has evaporated. Our experiences, to be of value, must make impressions deep and lasting.

Coleridge says that "to most men, experience is like the stern lights of a ship, which illumines only the track it has passed." And is it not too true? Do not our own hearts plead guilty? We have not been like the Indian, who, whenever he reached a dangerous bog in the swamp would put up a stake to mark the spot, and by this means guard his future movements.

Do we seek to deepen the impression which our experiences are calculated to produce by looking at them in all their bearings? When we are tempted to commit sin and the voice of the inward monitor warns us of our danger in season to prevent our fall, do we trace out in our thoughts what would have been the consequence of yielding in its effects upon our own lives, and upon the lives of our neighbors? Do we consider the joy and peace that is preserved to us; do we think of the strength and purity of character that is built up by thus resisting the siren voice of sin; or do we hang our experience as a stern light to illumine the past and turn our faces unto the future to face new dangers, walking in the dark shadows which our forgotten experiences have made?

Let us now consider more particularly the Experience Meetings, and how to conduct them—in other words, how to make them a success.

It should be clearly understood at the outset that their success depends not so much on the method of conducting the meeting (although that is not to be despised) as upon the preparation of the members for it. This holds good of any meeting, but is especially true of the experience meeting. We may give an impromptu address on a given subject, but we cannot give an impromptu experience. Hence the special need of preparation in order to make an experience meeting a success. And if we find that our experience meetings are not as satisfactory as we desire we may be sure that there is something lacking in the individual experience of the members. But, it may be objected, are there not times when the individual life is devoid of any special experience, when the daily routine has gone calmly on without a ripple to disturb its smoothness? Yes, it is granted; but is *that* not an experience that we should rejoice in! and enquiringly meditate upon, that we may know the reason for the calm, and, if possible, perpetuate it? Life is a succession of experiences, sometimes coming with startling suddenness and force like the destructive tornado; sometimes with the softness of the zephyr, and because of the unobtrusiveness and apparent insignificance of the latter kind of experience it passes unnoticed or unheeded. We are too watchful for great experiences to take much notice of the simple but sweet and helpful experiences which are coming to us all the time. Forgetting that the grains of sand make the mountain, that the drops of water make the ocean, and that in like manner the little experiences accumulating day by day make the full, rich experience of strong Christian manhood and womanhood. And now it may be asked what is the need of an experience meeting since it is the experience rather than the meeting which is the essential thing. The experience meeting is needed because of the frailty of human nature. It is needed as a stimulus to our experience. What we can do at any time, or when we feel like doing it, will probably not be done at all, unless it lies directly in the line of our inclination.

In a recent experience meeting a young sister testified to the value of the experience meeting in nearly these words : " The experience meeting has made me more watchful over my daily life." In a brother's diary the following sentence is found : "The memory of last month's experience in yielding to temptation, together with earnest prayer, kept me from flagrant sin to-day." These are testimonies to the value of the experience meeting as a stimulus to the experience.

A word of warning may be proper at this point in regard to preparing for the experience meeting. It may not be needed ; if not, it will do no harm.

In relating our experience in the meeting it is not necessary that we enter into a detailed account of our experience, and certainly it is not necessary that our experience should always, or even often, be of a striking character; neither is it to be expected that it will always be satisfactory to ourselves. Such an impression of the experience meeting would be liable to beget in the minds of the younger members a spirit of insincerity which would be disastrous to spiritual growth and the development of Christian experience. In relating our experiences we must be natural and truthful. Difficulty is sometimes found in getting the members to take part in the experience meeting. It is felt by some that their experience is a personal matter, and concerns no one but themselves. This difficulty may be overcome by a little explanation of what is required by way of experience. No one is required to go into details. No one is required to give a lengthy experience. There is so much to be gained by taking part in an experience meeting that we ought to be willing to sacrifice our feelings somewhat. What if we have to humiliate ourselves sometimes ! It is he who humbleth himsel fthat shall be exalted. It is the proud heart that stumbleth by the way.

As to methods of conducting an experience meeting : there is but little room for method, and the method will require to be varied according to the make up of the Society. There is a Society where, at the close of the experience meeting, all kneel and several lead in prayer, with the idea of consecration prominently in mind ; this is a good plan. In some cases it might succeed well for the leader to call the roll and let each member as he answers to his name give his experience either in some appropriate verse of scripture or in his own words. This plan would insure the testimony of all, yet it might not in all cases be wise to adopt such a plan. Another feature of the experience meeting ought often to be the reading of such parts of the constitution as relate to our pledges to the Society, which are really pledges to God.

In conclusion If a man would be a strong, well balanced, progressive Christian he must be a man of deep, rich, abiding experience. If he would have a deep, rich, abiding experience he must set his experience constantly before him and not behind him. If he would set his experience before him he must at stated times marshal and review it, as a wise general marshals and reviews his army, that he may know its condition and efficiency. And so, as members of churches, and Societies of Christian Endeavor we need a set time for reviewing our experiences,—and such is found in the *experience meeting*.

WAYS AND MEANS OF ENLARGING THE WORK OF THE YOUNG PEOPLE'S SOCIETIES OF CHRISTIAN ENDEAVOR,

By W. J. Van Patten,

Of the First Congregational Church, Burlington, Vermont.

A recent issue of the Sunday School Times says, "There was never a time when so much was being done by the church, in its organized capacity, for the influencing and training of children, as in the present generation."

This is undoubtedly true, and that it is true, is good cause for new joy and fresh hope for the future of the church in every christian heart.

There was a time when the influence of parents, and the prevailing tone of society, was such that children grew up into the church almost perforce.

There was but little of the liberty of thought, and action, which is accorded to children of to-day, and little else save matters of the church to attract the attention of the rising generation ; and so it was natural for the children to accept the belief of the parents, and at the proper time, and in the orthodox way, be received to church fellowship. This required no special effort on the part of the church, except the teaching of the catechism, and bible texts. But the new life of the 19th century, with its myriads of newspapers, its railroads, telegraphs, and countless other influences, changed both parents and children. The old methods were no longer adequate, and the children of the church were too apt to become tne children of this world.

There has been a long transition period during which the church has hardly seemed to hold its own—its gains being largely wrought out in the fierce heat of revival movements instead of by the steady and continuous reception of its children to its bosom. Many noble and godly men have seen this tendency, and have thought and planned and prayed over it. To what purpose and with what blessing may be seen by looking at the wonderful work of the Sunday School, especially since working through the International Committee ; at the work of the Young Men's Christian Associations, which now surround the world, and at the development of Young People's Societies in almost every church denomination in the land.

To those of us that have been interested in the growth and work of the Young People's Societies of Christian Endeavor that work seems to be especially adapted to the winning and holding of children to the service of their Saviour. Its success, which we believe shows the mark of Divine favor and blessing, has been such that we should feel it our duty to do what we can to enlarge and extend its work.

In considering the question of ways and means of enlarging let us try and profit by the experience of others. Let us consider the work of other organizations whose work is analogous, and see if similar methods may not be adapted to our own needs.

The object of our Societies is declared in our constitution to be "to promote an earnest christian life among its members, to increase their mutual acquaintance, and to make them more useful in the service of God."

The organized work whose object seems nearest to this is that of the Young Men's Christian Associations. Their object is declared to be "to promote the moral, spiritual, and social welfare of young men."

Next is the Sabbath School, whose primary object is instruction in biblical truths.

The first step to be taken by us is somewhat different from any necessary to these organizations. We must first acquaint pastors and churches with our work and its results, and show them how it may be organized and set in motion. In the first part of this we must secure the cooperation of pastors who already have societies under their charge. These pastors, by frequent articles sent to the religious press, giving their opinion of the plans of the society, and especially reporting how it has operated in their own churches, will awaken a lively interest in the work. Already a good deal of work of this kind has been done, and those pastors that have had a share in it can testify to the wide-spread interest that has been manifested. But much more is needed, and it needs to be repeated over and over again, for there are many churches where they would be quite sure that our plans would never do for them, and only by reiterated statement, and by new and fresh testimony of the blessing of God, can they be convinced.

How shall we be sure of having this work done by the pastors?

I would suggest that an agreement be sent to every pastor from whose church we have received a report, and their signature be urgently requested. By signing this agreement each one shall be obliged to send to some one or more of the religious papers, during the year, at least two articles explanatory of the aims and methods of the Young People's Society of Christian Endeavor, and give an account of the work done by the one under their own charge. In no other way can the work be brought so thoroughly to the notice of christian people, and nothing will so surely inspire new and zealous work as the account of good work done. The pastors too, should, in their meetings, conferences, and conventions, make the work of the Young People's Societies one of the subjects of report and discussion. What our pastors say about us, if in praise, will be much more effectual than any thing we can do or say. By this means a desire for information will be awakened; hundreds of questions will be asked, statistics and reports called for, and opinions and advice solicited.

How shall this information be given, and these questions answered? Here we will feel our need of organization. There should be a committee on publication who should prepare papers and reports, and have them printed for distribution, giving all the particulars possible in regard to organization, method of work, the best means of attaining success under God's guidance, as demonstrated by past experience, and what snares and pitfalls to avoid.

The International Committee of the Young Men's Christian Association publish a great many documents of this kind, and we can not do better than to follow their example.

In every great work done through organized societies it is necessary in order to be successful to secure a real *esprit du corps* among individual members; each member must be brought to feel that the work is theirs, and that if it is successful a portion of the credit and praise is due to them; and if it fails, the stigma of failure is theirs too.

How strongly this spirit animates, to-day, the Sunday School, and the Christian Association work! It is what gives them their impetus and leads them on to greater and still greater triumphs. How is this spirit fostered and brought into disciplined, judicious, effective work ? How is it aroused in those who have it not, and revived and strengthened in those who have ? This Conference, I trust, will answer that question.

The most characteristic development of Sunday School work of recent years has been the frequent conferences and conventions held ; district, County, State, National and International—Union and denominational. Did you never see your delegate come home from those conventions filled with fresh zeal and earnestness ? Have not your Sabbath Schools been vastly benefited by it ? Indeed they have. In all Church work, Mission work and Christian Association work great dependence is placed upon this coming together to take counsel of each other, and to gather fresh courage and inspiration from hearing of the work and blessing of others. Then let us avail ourselves of this means of enlarging the work of our Societies.

We may not have a sufficient number of organized Societies, as yet, to hold conventions by themselves, but we need not wait for that. Let us invite, as we have to this conference, representatives from every church, and bring together as many as possible of young christians to explain and illustrate to them the working of our Societies. I would begin in the larger towns by getting a Union Meeting of the young people of the different churches, and discussing the various methods of work. Of course, most churches have some sort of a young people's society, and it is rather a delicate thing to ask them to change from their methods of work to ours. What we want is for them to conform so nearly that we may confer and work together in harmony and to the same end.

Next I would have a County Conference. One good, live, Society is all that is needed in order to call such a conference, and make it a success, too Ask all the churches to send representatives, and let capable persons explain the work. When a year has rolled around there would be many new Societies to send representatives to the second conference. State Conventions would follow in their turn, and then would come the grandest and best of all, this National Convention, with its reports from hundreds, yes, thousands of Societies. Would we not find that the reapers had gone forth to the harvest, and had garnered thousands of sheaves for the Master ? Would it not be a jubilee full of faith and joy and love ?

I believe these conferences would so fill us with the Spirit that we should go on from victory to victory. We may feel sure that not many would not go to such conferences without getting full of enthusiasm for the work, for where is the christian worker that does not delight in striving to bring children to their Saviour ? Now, enthusiasm is one of the grandest powers in the moral universe. It is always a companion of that faith which has been declared to be able to move mountains, and we may well hope and pray that there will be no limit to that which will be inspired for this cause.

But enthusiasm is often strong and urgent in those who unfortunately lack somewhat the capacity of wise judgment and careful planning. And in many, enthusiasm is too apt to be short lived if it meets with opposition or unexpected difficulties. If not wisely guided, mistakes will be made, and then the enthusiast becomes discouraged, and perhaps relapses into a fault finder and a thrower of cold water.

How shall we be saved from such, and how shall their first enthusiasm be kept alive, and made a steady and persistent force ? In the work of the Young Men's Christian Association the need of trained men of good judgment, of keen insight, and broad view, was early felt. It was provided for by the appointment of Secretaries of the International Committee, whose numbers have been added to until there are now eleven constantly employed in advising and helping the local associations.

These Secretaries are aided by State Secretaries in many of the States, so there is a large force of picked men who are ready to give advice or render assistance wherever it is necessary. Association work to-day is what it has been made by these men, and it is noted for its wisdom, and persistent enthusiasm. In Sunday School work the need of such directors has been felt, and in many denominations Sunday School Secretaries have been appointed and the good effect of their work has been plainly manifest.

It seems to me that it will be a great aid in enlarging the work of these societies to have paid secretaries, to go from church to church, explaining the objects and plans of the work, aiding in organizing, and advising how to overcome local and special difficulties. Especially will their help be needed in conferences and conventions. Young people's societies must of necessity be made up of inexperienced members, and in their conventions they will need the help of those of experience. The work will soon be of such magnitude that it will require the entire time and thought of those who would undertake to direct it. In giving this matter a good deal of thought, I have seen but one way to carry out this suggestion.

Our Societies differ from Christian Associations in this : we are denominational, while they are not. Work done for one of our Societies is done for one denomination, while work done for an Association is done for all denominations. No one person can work satisfactorily for all denominations, or can so divide his time and efforts as to do away with all cause for complaint. Then will not this work be of such importance as to warrant each denomination in appointing a special secretary to look after its interests and promote its growth ? I believe it soon will be, and that we should labor to that end. Let us ask our pastors to present the subject to their respective conferences, or conventions, and to urge that some action be taken. Possibly it may be well to have more Sunday School Secretaries, and have the same persons look after the interests of both organizations. Their work is so closely allied and their ultimate object being identical, there should be no clashing of interests. Another great help, when the Societies become sufficiently numerous and prosperous to sustain it, would be a periodical devoted to their interests ; one which the young people could feel was their paper, and which would keep them informed of what Societies were doing all over the country, and what ways of working were found most successful in winning souls. The Sunday School papers and the Association papers have done a work in educating the people in their respective lines whose importance can not be over-estimated. I believe we will need the same educating influence in our work, and that the stimulating effect that would result in many Societies, from a knowledge of good and successful work elsewhere, would give new zeal and life. The outpouring of the Holy Spirit in one place would be felt far and wide, and a unity of purpose would result that could not otherwise be obtained. We can not expect to avail ourselves at once of all these different ways of enlarging our work, and very likely some of them may not be found practicable, but we must have some definite aims towards which, as united organizations, we are working. If, as the result of this discussion and guided by the Divine Spirit, we can adopt some wise plans, we may feel sure our work will be owned and honored by our Lord. Let us then, trusting in His strength and wisdom, take a wide, far-reaching outlook, which shall embrace nothing less than the establishment of a Society of Christian Endeavor in every church in our broad land, and their working together in love and unity to advance the Kingdom of our God.

One division of this question—that of means—I have not left myself time to discuss. Sooner or later we shall need money to carry forward some part of our work, but I believe we may rest in perfect faith that when the time comes we shall receive what we need. No Christian work for the young, when rightly presented to Christian people, ever suffers for lack of means.

Let us then, in faith, hope and love, move forward to the work which we can not but feel that our Divine Master has given us to do.

THE RELATION OF THE SOCIETY TO THE SUNDAY SCHOOL.

By Hon. H. H. Burgess,

Of the St. Lawrence Street Society, Portland, Maine.

The Sabbath School, organized at first mainly to have the scholars commit scripture passages to memory and recite them, with such general remarks as the pastor or those appointed for the purpose might make, has come now step by step to be a great and powerful auxiliary to the church in leading the young, not only to understand the Scripture, but by its organization to interest the young in Christian work. These improvements have been largely brought about through the prayerful and thoughtful interest of those who have felt that very largely to the young must we look for the building up of our churches. And in this line of progress we have the establishment of this Society,—and now the question comes, What can we do for the Sunday School scholar?

1st. In its organization and business rules, unlike our usual young people's meeting, which we commence and give up at pleasure, we endeavor to have this Society a permanent institution, governed by rules which are binding on all its members; each one is expected and required to add to its interest, and by so doing, to their advancement in the Christian life.

2d. In its social nature it appeals to them, and through its harmless amusements shows them the social side of a religious life. By our rules, half an hour at the close of each meeting is devoted to social conversation, and occasionally a sociable bringing the young together has proven a valuable help in holding those who have reached that age when they consider themselves too old to go longer to the Sabbath School.

3d. The opportunity it offers to give expression to Christian thought and feeling. There are very many among our Sunday School scholars who know the truth, and know the principles and doctrines of religion, who have never felt that they could give expression to their feelings in our regular church prayer meetings, who have found these young people's meetings a place where they could, with more freedom, speak of their experience in or a desire for a religious life. Here are those in like circumstances with themselves, desiring to promote an earnest Christian life, and it is not strange that very soon they should be glad to speak of this desire where at first it was done from a sense of obligation.

4th. The opportunity it gives to personally present the claims of Christ upon their companions. Here they meet, on common ground, young hearts warm with the love of Christ. The earnestness of the prayer meeting just upon them, what better time to speak to their young companions than now of their desire for their salvation? How often has the half-hour at the close of the meeting been thus spent, and with what blessed results?

I have briefly stated some of the ways that this Society can be, and has been, a very great help to the Sabbath School scholar in leading him onward and upward to a true Christian life. It does not aim to supplant the Sabbath School in teaching the truths of the Bible, but rather to give an opportunity to exemplify them in an earnest Christian life. Sabbath School teachers should be found among its most earnest advocates ; and, if, in every school in our land, such a Society should be organized and sustained, I am sure the church would reap a rich harvest in warm young hearts given to Christ and the Church. I have heard Mr. Moody say that the Young Men's Christian Association was the right arm of the church ; may we not as truthfully say that this Society, raised up at this time for a special work, is the right arm of the Sabbath School?

WHO MAY BECOME MEMBERS OF THE YOUNG PEOPLE'S SOCIETY OF CHRISTIAN ENDEAVOR?

By Rev. S. Winchester Adriance,

Pastor of the Congregational Church, Woodfords, Maine.

I am to discuss a very large topic. In a certain sense it involves the great question of success or failure of such a movement as that of the Societies of Christian Endeavor. It is undoubtedly true that if any Societies have come to an untimely end, there has either been heresy or negligence on this subject. It is by no means an easy question to answer.

1. What are the limits as *to age?* This is by no means an easy question to solve in theory and still harder in practice. Dangers are met on two sides. If Societies are confined in membership to those under twenty-three there will be lacking a maturity which is very much needed for permanent

success. And yet, on the other hand, many a sad pastor has laid such a Society tenderly away in its grave, because it had too many members over thirty years old. Douglass Jerold says "a man is only as old as he feels," and that being true, as it unquestionably is, some even over forty may be acceptable and freshening members. But if we keep in clear view the design of these Societies, there will practically be no more difficulty here than in every question. This Society is not designed for the older ones, but to organize the young, to promote their interest in religious work and life, and to train them to take the places of the older ones as they shall drop away.

In the light of this design, what is best? It will be readily seen that there are dangers very grave if older people are members in large number. The very design is defeated. It is a hard thing at best to make our boys and girls feel their responsibilities when they have become Christians. They are only too ready to shift them. Those who are now active workers in the church are so by a sort of survival of the fittest. They have come to the front in spite of difficulties. These Societies have a wonderful mission in propping up the weak consciences. If older ones are members in considerable numbers, what is the consequence? The timid, shrinking Harry Jones, and the bashful Susie Black, come into the meetings. They do want to work for Jesus, but they have no confidence. And when they look around there are Deacons Smith and Jones, and brothers Dean and Adams. So these wait till Deacon Smith has spoken, and he always says such grand, good things, that the word or two which Harry could say seems poorer and poorer, and so their courage oozes away little by little, and they become silent members. And this, in spite of the strict rules, expecting every one to take part.

There is another danger: that these older ones will too often and too largely assume the part of fathers in the faith, and scold, and warn and instruct. The gift of advice is a gift that very few excel in, and one which those few need to get steeped in the love of Christ. One such talk of advice I have known, again and again, to kill a meeting worse than a dozen ridiculous blunders of a young Christian's first attempt.

And this design of organizing and energizing the young is hindered by the unconscious assumption on the part of the older ones, of the control of the Society.

It is not in any sense the wish to debar the older ones from spiritual privileges. It is interesting and blessed to be in meetings where there is the warmth and freshness of the new life. But does not God call us to make a sacrifice here for the young, if by so doing we can help make them stalwart workers for Christ? *Ordinarily*, then, the membership of these Societies ought to consist of those between thirteen and thirty.

And yet, I remark again, I should be very sorry if none of the brethren and sisters between thirty and forty, and even older, belonged to the Society. A few of these more mature members are needed, else our Societies may dwindle into juvenile Societies. The young need to feel that the older ones are interested in them, and the older ones need some freshening intercourse with the young. Not only so, but the presence of some of these older ones will tend to give maturity to the young faith. There are always one or two older ones in whom the young have much confidence, and these may help in encouragement and advice, and many other ways.

2. Again, the pastor should always be a member, and present at every meeting. His position in the church work is *sui generis*. He is superintendent of every branch of church work, and this makes it needful that he should be there. There is no supervision like personal supervision. But he is more than a superintendent. He is the pastor, and that grand old word—*shepherd*—includes the personal care of every age and character. The good shepherd knows the names of all his lambs ; a good pastor knows the names of every young person in his church. It gave Napoleon a great deal of that wonderful hold over his troops, if what is said is true—that he knew the name of every member of his troops. There is not one reason only why the pastor should be in the meeting, but many. By his presence he draws them to him—they think of him as knowing them. By his presence he gets a view of their character and needs, and is able to reach them. By his presence he will give the meetings a tone which they will not have without him. By his presence he is himself kept young, for their faith reacts on him. No pastor can afford to delegate this duty to another. The Brooklyn bridge may go up by the engineer watching it from his sick room, through a telescope. A general may sit on his horse and send his commands into the smoke, by his aide. But a pastor must be in the midst of every fight in these days.

Again, I would have children join as early as they can attend regularly. There has sometimes been the objection that the Societies lead to clannishness. It is a sufficient answer to this to point to the natural clannishness of life. Young men have natural friendships ; old men draw together ; children trip along side by side. But this is not clannishness. And if, from the man of forty down to the girl of ten, all ages are represented, there will be no caste. I am well aware that in many communities, especially in the country, it is impracticable for many children to come. I only repeat "if they can let them join." It will help them, and besides, they are just as good teachers to-day as when the Master set a child before His disciples as their text.

4. I say again : I would have every one who is trying to live a Christian life be an active member. This is particularly necessary because some have claimed that only church-members should be active members. It has been objected that any other method would make the Society a substitute for the church. It does seem to me that this continually resurrected bug-bear is like the hobgoblins of my childhood, in the closets and dark corners ; they only exist in our fears and fancies.

Let us go back to our design. Is it not the formation and development of Christian character ? We know that transition stage which young Christians pass through just after conversion. They do not feel strong, and often hardly know whether they are Christians or not. We remember Bunyan's picture of "Christian," how very soon after his start from the city of Destruction he fell into the slough of Despond. Then while floundering there a shining one came and lifted him out. Now, this Society is the shining one. Its membership receives even a Pliable, and many a poor Pliable, helped by this membership, through Christ, has been brought afterward into t e church. It is of utmost importance, then, that the admission of members be so simple that it will bring in every one, however weak his faith, to this Society.

5. I am very much impressed, let me say again, with the importance of admitting associate members, and endeavoring to enlarge that membership. I have found that it has been of great help. They have realized that in joining as associate members they have more than half committed themselves, and often the succeeding steps have been taken very quickly.

6. Finally, I mention in a few words, those who should not belong :

1. All who do not wish to work for Christ.
2. All who are not willing to help the young.
3. All who cannot peaceably work with others.
4. All who cannot talk briefly.
5. All who are born critics, and are nothing if not critical.
6. All who are not willing to attend constantly.
7. All who are not willing to make any sacrifice, whatever, for Christ.

OUR RULES—HOW STRICTLY SHOULD THEY BE ENFORCED?

BY W. H. PENNELL, ESQ.,

Of the Williston Society, Portland, Maine.

This may be answered in a single word,—literally,—for since there is no verbal reservation in any of the rules or requirements, there should be no mental reservation in the agreement to observe these rules.

What are our rules? The Preamble to our Constitution says that "the object of this Society is to promote an earnest Christian life among its members, to increase their mutual acquaintance and make them more useful in the service of God." To accomplish these results it is necessary to have some rules; and these rules are the distinguishing characteristics of our Society. One of these rules—and the one which is said by some to be the hardest to observe—is in relation to the prayer-meetings. "It is expected that all the active members will be present at every meeting, unless detained by absolute necessity, and that each one will take some part, however slight, in every meeting."

The object of this rule is to promote an earnest Christian life among the members. We would not be understood as saying that attending prayer-meeting, and speaking in meeting, is all there is in a Christian life; but we do say that the person, young or old, who makes no public profession of religion will not be very useful in the service of God.

In our service of God we are to be witnesses for Christ ; and we make a promise to Him that at each meeting we will witness for Him,—it is a *solemn promise*.

Just as sacred as an honorable business man regards his pledged word in commercial transactions should we regard our word, voluntarily given, to attend and support these meetings. Yes, and *more* sacred even, for this is a religious vow ; and God is a witness to, and a party in, every religious vow.

There is necessarily something left to the discretion and conscience of every member of the Society ; but, let each one beware how he abuses or strains his conscience. It is a terrible thing to tamper with conscience. For an active member to stay away, or keep silent in one of these meetings, when he might be present and support it, is an acted *lie*. Let us not call it by any milder name. Neglect of these obligations is just as dishonorable and may be far more harmful in an older Christian, than in a boy or girl who has just began a Christian life.

We do not expect that those who put their hand to the plough will turn back or that they will "run well for a season," and then will take their places with the silent Christians. This enlistment is for *life*. Having agreed to this rule we cannot break our promise, unless, like Annanias, we would keep back a part. You remember he promised to give all he had, and his terrible fate is a warning to each one of us who breaks his pledged word.

We desire to be more useful in the service of God that we may win souls to Christ. To do this effectually we must be consistent ; we must look to our influence upon others—especially in the fulfilment of our promises. You may be accompanied to the prayer-meeting by some young friend for whom you have been praying—one whom you would gladly see brought into the Society, and so into communion with Christ. They know the obligation you have voluntarily assumed, and, if you sit silent, will it not more surely drive the Holy Spirit from the careless one than though you attempt to speak and utterly fail to express the thoughts you would ? It is not only for the influence upon others that we should be faithful to our promises, but upon ourselves, for the one who turns back from one duty will find it hard to recover the character or work he has lost. I know many of you will say "I would gladly take part but I do not know what to say." Well, begin if you please with a selection of Scripture or from your favorite devotional book, but don't stop there ; try to think thoughts worthy of the Master, and you will find words to express your thoughts.

The promise is to you "Seek and ye shall find," "ask and ye shall receive," and to you the assurance, "Blessed are they who hunger and thirst, for they shall be filled," and when God fills you then you are ready to fill others.

I have spoken at length upon this rule, for it is one I think that should be most carefully observed. You may ask, what is "absolute necessity" that will prevent attending the weekly meeting ? You must decide this question between yourself and your God. When you attempt to decide the matter prayerfully you may be sure you will be guided aright.

And so with our Committee work. The rules require that the various committees shall do certain work ; upon the performance of this work depends in a great measure the success of the Society. The Prayer Meeting Committee should prepare a subject and provide a leader for each meeting. The Social Committee should provide for the mutual acquaintance, and for proper entertainment at all the social gatherings ; the Lookout Committee should very carefully observe the rule for the admission of new members, that no one may be brought in who does not understand these rules, and will not cheerfully live up to them, and they must just as earnestly and conscientiously look out for the weak and careless ones, and, if any grow cold, their duty is plain to try to reclaim them and bring them back.

Are our rules too strict ? We can only say the agreement is voluntary ; but once assumed, these rules should be as binding as the rules of the church.

It is customary to call those persons Christians whose names are on the church books, though they may be known as such in no other way. Let us, in our Society, try to show the world that we believe Christians say what they mean, and mean what they say, and that they interpret literally the promise they make to their Master, and that we will try, by His help, to strictly adhere to them.

HOW MAY YOUNG LADIES ASSIST IN THIS WORK?

By Miss Ada Sewall,

Of the Second Parish Society, Portland, Maine.

The question has been asked, "What can the young ladies do ?" The answer to this depends upon the spirit with which they enter the Society and the way they look upon its work.

If one joins because she thinks she must, with mind fully made up that it will be impossible for her to take part in any of the active work, and that all any one ought to expect of her is to come to the meetings and, perhaps, say a verse from the Bible, it is safe to say such an one can do but little, at least, until she has a change of purpose.

If it is true, "That we are able because we think we are able," it is equally true that we are *not* able when we *think* we are not. But if there is one with an earnest desire in her heart to do something for Him who has done so much for her, who is willing to undertake any little service for H's sake, then this Society offers abundant opportunities for work. Only let the heart be right and the time and ability will not be wanting.

It is said that women possess, in a high degree, the ability to make themselves agreeable, to inspire enthusiasm and courage in others. If this be true, here is the opportunity for using that gift, which God has given them, by creating a clear, bright atmosphere wherever they are, and by doing their work in such a glad, happy spirit that others shall feel the contagion, and before they know it, shall find themselves also actively engaged.

Dear young ladies, be enthusiastic. As you go about among your friends speak a word for the "Society of Endeavor"; put as much heartiness into what you say as you would in talking to your art society, your literary work, or a very delightful excursion you have planned for next summer. You do not know how much weight your word may have. But do not allow words of discouragement to pass your lips, they are stumbling-blocks for others to fall over. There is nothing so paralyzing to every effort for good as cold discouraging words, and half-hearted sympathy.

If you are discouraged—and who is not at times—keep it to yourselves till the sun shines through your fog; or go to the President, or some one whom your words will not hurt. Or, better still, take it to Him who made the heart and knows all its crookedness and trials, and then, if things are going wrong do the right thing yourself, showing others also how to do it, saying nothing about the wrong, but leaving it with God. Then there are the girls whose hearts you can win by making them feel that you are one with them, by showing them that the religion of Jesus Christ is one for boys and girls as well as for grown people, that it is one they can carry into their homes, their lessons, their pleasures. You can make them see, not by word only but by deed, that the girl or woman who has Christ in her life is more truly happy, in every way, than she who has not. Go to their sociables; join in their games; do not be afraid of your dignity; an hour or two so spent will do you good.

Then you are to show them how they can begin to work by setting them some easy task. Try and make them feel that responsibility is not something to be shunned, but something to be gladly taken up. For duties faithfully performed always bring their own reward in a sense of satisfaction, and in the strengthening of the whole character.

The Society of Christian Endeavor is a body of young men and women, boys and girls, who have bound themselves together to work for Christ, to help one another, and to gather in those who have no religious interest, and to show them the right way. In order to further this end they bind themselves by their written word that they will do all in their power to advance the Society, to be present at and take part in, every meeting.

Some join apparently under the impression that if the meetings are not as interesting as they think they ought to be, or there are more interesting ones elsewhere, they are absolved from their pledge. This is not so, neither is there anything in the pledge which frees young ladies from the promise they make that they will take part in every meeting.

We have in our ranks teachers, who are accustomed to stand every day before from thirty to sixty or more boys and girls, not to speak of the Committeemen and visitors, and talk to them on almost every subject, from the "Hyssop that springeth out of the wall," to the great bodies which circle about us in space and of which so little is really known. They give to their scholars not only what they have taken from the store-houses of other minds, but thoughts which God has given them for their own. Stand beside one of these teachers in her class-room, as she gives an object lesson or leads her scholars along higher paths; there is no fear, no hesitancy, no stammering. The words come easily, and carry conviction because they are given with heartiness. Follow them into their Sabbath School classes, or into the Bible class, if they are scholars, and then into the sociable and they are the same as in their class-rooms; but let the four walls of our little vestries close them in, and they become dumb. Why is it? Is it because God, who gives to all liberally and has given to them knowledge in regard to His works of creation, has withheld from them all thoughts of Himself, His word, and practical Christianity ? Is it that fear has fallen upon them ? Is the little company, which has come together with an earnest desire to be helped and to help, more formidable than the class-room full of scholars provided with the full armor of criticism ?

Surely, more than facts in regard to the world of art and science, do the boys and girls need facts in regard to right living. A few words condensed, if necessary, into one sentence ; a suggestion ; a hint, such as the minister cannot give in his sermons ; how helpful they are. A simple question thrown out into a meeting often does as much good as a whole volume.

But there are many girls and young ladies, who are not teachers, not accustomed to express themselves before a number, and who feel they dare not make an attempt for fear they should fail. To such I would say, try and put yourself out of your own sight ; think of Him who shrank from no suffering if perchance He might save some. Your word, poor and unworthy as it may seem to you, may be just the word that some one else needs.

Phillips Brooks in one of his Easter sermons says, " How good it would be for some of us if this bright Easter Day would show us immortality and so set some of us free. There are some things you are afraid to do, some right word you are afraid to speak, some attempt to be useful in some little enterprising way from which you shrink, out of a fear of what people will say about it, out of a fear of the little world. You would get rid of that fear instantly if you realized your immortality. What is there in scorn or criticism that dies the day it is born to terrify the man who is to live forever ? He is free. He has entered into the glorious liberty of the children of God."

Do not think that this Society advocates pushing young people forward or making them self-sufficient, arrogant, and conceited. Far otherwise ; but we believe that an unselfish giving of one's self in word and deed tends rather to keep the heart pure. By sharing the one or two holy thoughts with others they become doubled, even as the loaves broken in our Saviour's hands.

I once came upon a little spring nestled in among the mosses and ferns. All about grew tall shrubs whose branches bending low were cooled by its spray. Towering above the shrubs stood stately trees looking down upon the little spring, while the wind blowing through their branches made grand, sweet music. The water of the spring was clear as crystal, one could look through it to the clear white sand on the bottom. And, though it was constantly bubbling up, bathing the roots of the shrubs and ferns, it never grew muddy ; and, though its song was merry and constant, it made no discord with the music of the pines ; but there was harmony in all the woods.

So will it be in the church when all, not only the older ones, but the boys and girls, the young men and women, shall have their own places and their own individual work to do—a work of praise to God and blessing to others.

HOW A SOCIETY MAY BE ESTABLISHED, AND WHAT IT MAY ACCOMPLISH.

The Experience of the Kirk Street Society, Lowell, Mass.

By Frank W. Hall, Lowell.

The Young People's Society of Christian Endeavor of Kirk Street Congregational Church, at Lowell, send a cordial Christian greeting to this representative assembly of Young People's Societies.

Our organization is the only one of its kind in the city. We have not yet become sufficiently strong and well organized to make any deep impression upon the young people in the various churches of Lowell; and, besides, many of them already have Societies more or less similar to our own. We hope, by the time for holding the next Convention, that some of these organizations may be induced to alter their name and join with us in sending delegates. Failing in this, we shall make earnest efforts to cause the establishing of Young People's Societies of Christian Endeavor in the churches where the young people do not conduct their religious work under the direction of an organization.

Just three months ago this evening (on the 7th of March,) the initiatory steps were taken toward the foundation of the Kirk Street Society, and one week later a permanent organization was effected, at an enthusiastic meeting of about forty-five young people, nearly all of whom signed the Constitution, and only one as an associate member. We adopted, and have had printed, the same Constitution as that of the Williston Society. At a recent meeting, however, it was amended so as to provide for the election of a treasurer, and also for the auditing of his accounts by the vice-president.

Our membership, as the name of our organization implies, is composed of young people, though there are a few middle-aged members, who probably consider themselves young. It is made up of recruits from the Church, the Society and the Sabbath School, and there are now signed to the Constitution the names of seventy-six members.

When, during the first few weeks of our organization, notices were read at the sessions of the Sunday School, and invitations extended to young people to become members it was intimated that we wished to make the Society and its meetings exclusively for young people. The object toward which we aim in being thus exclusive is that we shall feel more free to speak and to take part in leading the meetings.

The young people now conduct the monthly sociables at our church, and those who have previously had the care of them are very much pleased with the change; yet they stand ready to assist and advise us. We do not intend that the sociables shall be any less interesting, at least, than they have heretofore been. Sociables exclusively for young people have not yet been inaugurated.

As to our meetings, they have been a perfect success. There has not yet been seen the least embarrassment, and with lagging we have not become acquainted. We occupy the hour from 7.45 to 8.45 each Tuesday evening. Some meetings could easily be made to extend even another hour because of the deep interest taken. These weekly gatherings are very helpful to the young people in a spiritual way; and by their aid, the acquainting of the members one with another, makes more progress in one month than it has in the past done in a year.

From this Society two have already joined the church on profession of their faith; and you must bear in mind that we have not yet begun to work in full earnest.

A point of special importance, we think, is the relation of the Pastor to the Society. Our pastor is deeply and affectionately interested with us in our work, and it is owing to his indefatigable efforts that we have succeeded so well. He attends the meetings regularly, unless unavoidably detained, and his presence and his words of encouragement and advice have been of the utmost importance in aiding to ·ust in us thus far. His affection for the young people is heartily reciprocated, and we deem ourselves fortunate in having one to direct our efforts who was so intimately connected with the founders of this exceedingly happy method of promoting the religious welfare of young people.

We have found that the organizing of this Society has tended to increase our interest in the Sabbath School. It awakens such a deep concern in religious work that the Sunday School must in time profit thereby to a very perceptible extent.

The relations of our Society to the church are exceedingly pleasant. I know of no better phrase to express the feelings with which the older members of the church regard our Society than that they are heartily delighted with our work, and are equally ready to render assistance. At the outset, some of them pledged financial support, that our Society might not fail from want of funds. Thus commenced and supported by the church, we hope in the future to accomplish much for the cause of the Lord Jesus Christ among the young.

REPORT OF THE SECRETARY OF THE CONFERENCE OF YOUNG PEOPLE'S SOCIETIES OF CHRISTIAN ENDEAVOR.

MR. J. W. STEVENSON,

Of the Second Parish Society, Portland, Maine.

The Society of Christian Endeavor is the result of a felt need in the church. In the spring of 1881 the subject of recruiting the churches from among the young was discussed for several successive sessions of the ministers' meeting in Boston. It was felt that the churches were not increasing in numbers and power, and that the young were growing up without a saving knowledge of Jesus.

The subject was referred to a committee composed of Rev. Messrs. Wm. Barrows, D. D., R. R. Meredith and A. E. Dunning. This committee have endorsed the Society of Christian Endeavor as one means by which the desired end may be reached. The desired end is two-fold : first, to bring the gospel of Jesus Christ home to the hearts of the young with converting power, and second, to give the young converts something to do. And this latter is perhaps the more important work of the Society, because it provides a work which the young convert can do. Now has this truly good work and great need been met by the work of the Society? Let the reports which come from the Societies speak in response to this question. A pastor said this morning, "You may set against our report these words, 'Surprisingly successful!'" The pastor referred to further adds in a brief written report, "Soon after the formation of the Society a quiet religious interest was awakened, in connection with which there have been over forty conversions, with several still interested." In another church about forty young people ranging from 12 to 15 years of age were converted, and it became a serious question what to do to keep them from getting out of the good way. Some one discovered the Rev. Mr. Clark's book, "The Children and the Church," and the result was the formation of a Society of Christian Endeavor.

Another Society reports that the church felt the need of doing something to promote the zeal and fervor which follows conversion. The retiring president writes on "June 12, '82, the first experience meeting was held, and it will long be remembered by those who attended. Many thought it the best meeting ever held in our lecture room."

The agent of the Y. M. C. A. of Vermont in visiting one of the churches there heard of the organization for the first time, and was much pleased, saying that where there were no Y. M. C. As. these Societies would well supply their place. They do the work, however, that the Y. M. C. A. cannot do.

Time and space will not allow us to give all the encouraging words that come from the Societies. A few words here about the developing power of the Societies. Again the words from the Societies shall bear the evidence. "Marked development in prayer and remark, showing that it is a training school for the church," says one Society. Says another, "Much more interesting than the old way of conducting Young People's Meetings"; and another, "Attendance at Young People's Meetings have nearly trebled; several will soon join the church." And another, "Interest manifested among young people a surprise"; and another, and this is in the words of the pastor, "Brings pastor into close intercourse with the young people. Work done, very important." And still another, "The wonder is that we did not realize before what a force of young people we have"; and another, "Experience meeting grows in interest"; and yet once more on this point, "A year ago the time was taken up at each meeting by eight or ten members, about the same each time; now it is not uncommon for seventy-five voices to take part. We now get the best testimonies from those lips which hitherto had been closed." Is there any evidence of developing power here? Is there not abundant material in these Societies to do grand work for the Great Head of the church in winning young hearts from the kingdom of darkness and planting them through the grace of God in the kingdom of light and life? Growing, helpful, full of hope, faith in the work,—these are some of the terse additional testimonies to the value of the work.

It may not be out of place to add briefly as suggestions some channels and methods of work that come to us through the reports. A Society in Providence is engaged in establishing a public reading room for its section of the city. Another supplies wall leaflets for its members; another has established a reading circle. The Society in Oakland, Cal., have three classes of members, the beginners, the communion class and the young members' class

And now before closing we present you with the figures, which show, to some degree, the extent of the work. It is estimated that there are about three hundred Societies in the United States and Canada. We have, however, reports from only fifty-six.

The number of reports would undoubtedly have been greater had it been more generally known that a Conference was to be held and that reports were desired. These Societies extend from Maine to California, with a few in Canada. Of those reported, Maine has 17; Wisconsin 3; Vermont 4; Connecticut 3; New Hampshire 2; Illinois 2; New York 5; Rhode Island 2; New Jersey 2; Michigan 1; Massachusetts 11; Missouri 2; Iowa 1; and California 1.

They are divided among the denominations as follows: Congregational 45; Free Baptist 1; Baptist 3; Presbyterian 3; Dutch Reform 1; Methodist 2; Christian 1. It is hoped by another year the denominations will be more equally represented.

The largest and oldest is Williston of this city, organized February 2, '81, having now 164 members. The next in size is Oakland, Cal., with 148 members. The smallest is Acton, Me., which has 6 members. This comparison is not made to discourage the small Society but rather to commend its courage and inspire its zeal by our warm sympathy and prayers. This plucky little Society is working its way into the hearts of the people. We pray God it may succeed; and it will, if it holds on, for the Lord is with even two or three that are gathered in His name. We say to you Society of Acton go on in the name of the Lord conquering and to conquer.

The youngest Society is that of Milton, N. H., which, notwithstanding its extreme youth, only three days old, sends us a delegate to-day in the person of its pastor. We say its pastor, for the minister is the pastor of the Society as well as of the church. There is one Society which reports 26 active members and 35 church members ; another 68 active members and 80 church members, thus showing that a number of the church members are associate members. It is difficult to conceive of a reason why church members should not be active members They may do as good work as associate as they would if active members, under pledge to keep the rules, but the probability is they will not. Experience is to the contrary. We ought not to shrink from promises, although they may entail some self-sacrifice. Self-sacrifice is always in the way of gracious rewards. It is the spirit of the Gospel.

Of the 56 Societies reported, 5 were organized in 1881, 24 in 1882, 27 in 1883. That is, in six months, 5 of the 27 were organized in May, and 1 in June as already stated. Mark the steady advance. If it is an indication of what is to be, what may we not expect in the future as we see the value of the work already done.

The total membership reported by the 56 Societies is as follows ;

Active members,..2018
Associate members, ... 673
Members not classified,.. 179
                                                            ——
                                                          2870

Of this number 1398 are church members, and of these 253 have been added to the church from the Societies, or as near as can be estimated about 18 per cent. in the average time of not much more than one year. Truly a very gratifying result. And what is the lesson which it brings to us ? Not as some have been too ready to think that the church is failing in its usefulness. This work is a church work. The lesson is briefly this : that the heart in the freshness of youth is more susceptible to impression than later in life, and that any agency which will bring the church into direct contact with the young is an agency of the highest value. Such an agency we believe the Society of Christian endeavor to be.

OF CHRISTIAN ENDEAVOR.

NAME.	City or Town.	State.	Denom.	When Org.	Act. Mem.	Ass. Mem.	Ch. Mem.	Uniting With Church.	REMARKS.
Cumberland Centre,	Cumberland,	Maine.	Cong.	Feb'y 1, '83.	16	3	18		Interest good.
First Ch. W. St. Louis,	W. St. Louis,	Mo.	Cong.						Not yet organized.
	Shelburn	Mass.	Cong.	June, '82.	21	12	19	5	Organization helpful.
West End,	Portland	Maine.	Cong.	April 26, '82.	32	3	14	8	Meetings well attended.
Bucksport,	Bucksport.	Maine.	Cong.	Jan'y 25, '83.	26	38	35		Meetings very interesting.
	Acton	Maine.	Cong.	April 20, '83.	6		5		
Norway,	Norway,	Maine.	Cong.	Feb'y 20, '83.	28	5	20	5	Exp meeting grows in interest.
Fredonia,	Fredonia.	N. Y.	Pres.	Mar. 28, '83.	30	40	18	7	2 on probation.
	Shelton	Conn.	Meth.	Sept., '82.	20		15	4	A great success, attendance nearly trebled; several soon to join Ch. 10 act.
	Grafton	Mass.	Cong.	Oct. 22, '82.	16		16		and 8 associate not yet a gm-d.
Emmanuel Church,	Boston	Mass.	Cong.	Feb'y 27, '83.	65	19	43		At'ndance from 30 to 40, baptise¹ 6
Upton,	Upton	Mass.	Cong.	Feb'y 4, '83	25	22	22	3	[your. people but only 2 mem. of Soc.
Kankakee,	Kankakee	Illinois.	Bap.	Sept., '82.	20	11	19	2	Great faith in the organization.
Rockland,	Scituate	R. I.	Chr.	Nov. 22, '81.	13	7	13		
Brandon,	Brandon	Vermont.	Cong.	Oct., '82 '83.	13	15	15		Meetings well attended but lack of freedom in prayer and remarks.
	Monticello	Iowa.	Cong.	Nov. 26, '83.	22	16	20	1	
	Burlington	Vermont.	Cong.	Dec. 5, '81.	84	15	77	27	
	Jamestown.	N. Y.	Cong.	Feb'y 23, '83.	34	8	21	2	
Concord	Concord	Mass.	Cong.	April 24, '83.	32	6	31		
Young Chr. Circle,	Wellsley	Mass.	Cong.	Jan'y 22, '82.	45	21	35		
	New Haven	Conn.	Cong.	May 6, '83.	66		37		
	Oakland	Cal.	Cong.	Aug. 24, '82.	102	102	46	16	See very flourishing.
Williston,	Portland	Maine.	Cont.	Feb'y 2, '81.	147	17	105	8	
2d Parish,	Portland	Maine.	Cong.	Feb'y, '82	54	9	50	48	
1st Baptist,	Portland	Maine.	Bap.	Feb'y 23, '83.	55	98	36		Results very encouraging.
St. Lawrence St.	Portland	Maine.	Cong.	Dec. 1, '81.	47	30	38	15	An instrument to bless the Church.
Y. P. Chr. Union,	Portland	Maine.	F. Bap.	Oct. 29, '82	61	32	51	10	Helpful soc, Intel. and Spiritually.
Christian Workers,	Woodfords	Maine.	Cong.	Oct. 19, '82.	63	38	48	18	Surprisingly successful.
	Racine	Wis.	Cong.	Nov. 14, '82.	77		13	6	Faith in the Work.
	St. Johnsbury	Vermont.	Cong.		61		50	4	
Christian Helpers,	New Haven	Conn.	Cong.	April 8, '83.	56	6	22		
Y. P. Chr. Association,	Great Falls	N. H.	Cong.	April 3, '83.	44	4	12		Growing and well attended.
	Washington Heights.	Illinois.	Cong.	April 29, '82.	24	9			
	Boscobel	Wis.	Cong.	Sept. 6, '82.	22		11	1	
Judson,	Chuffenango	N. Y.	Bap.	July 8, '82.	46	13	20	3	Aver. Atten. 25.
	Palmyra.	N. Y.	Pres.	May 22, '82.	68	3	45		
	Rochester	N. Y.	Pres.	April 25, '82.	38	55	80	7	
	Providence	R. I.	Cong.	Oct. 3, '82	23	4			
Plymouth Ch.	Belville	Dut. Ref	Feb'y 28, '83.	18	17	19	8	Aver. Atten. 30.
	Litchfield	Mich.	Cong.	April 29, '83.	42	12			
	Newburyport.	Mass.	Cong.	Oct., '81.	10	1			6 or more desiring admission.
	Rockland	Mass.	Meth.	May 29, '83.	59	7	6	2	
West End,	Portland.	Maine.	Cong.	Dec. 26, '82.	40	8	37	19	
1st Cong'l,	Limington	Maine.	Cong.	Mar. 3, '83.	21	13	20	14	
	Freeport.	Maine.	Cong.	March, '82.	50	32	30		
Union Ch.,	Auburn.	Maine.	Cong.	Nov. 10, '82.	20	1	15		
Crescent St.,	Kennebunk	Maine.	Cong.	May 24, '83.	23	14	14		
No. Ave. Ch.	Biddeford.	Maine.	Cong.	May, '83.	35	35			
College St.	Cambridge	Mass.	Cong.	Nov. 8, '83.	35	30	36		
	Auburndale.	Vermont.	Cong.					2	
	Lowell	Mass.	Cong.	March, '83.	69	7	43		
	Wilton.	N. H.	Cong.	June 4, '83.	17		4		
	St. Louis	Mo.	Cong.	Nov. 2, '82.	45	14	40	3	
	Chester	N. J.	Cong.	April 11, '82.	29		15	5	
	Beloit.	Wis.	Cong.	Oct., '82.	51	56	36		
					2,018	673	1,396	253	179 unclassified members.

What some Societies Have Accomplished.

The most practical and helpful words which can be spoken concerning any such organization as the Society of Christian Endeavor are the details of actual experience, which show what has been accomplished and how it has been done. Here are not theories, but facts. We give a few pages of extracts from the hundreds of letters received from those engaged in this work for the young, hoping they may show how practicable these methods have been found amid many varying circumstances.

From Woodfords, Maine.

The Society in my church was started in October under very unfavorable circumstances, at a time of religious dearth, and with scarcely a young man as member. After a trial of ten months, now I can say that it has done this much :

First—It has made the young people, many of whom were idle before, earnest helpers of the pastor in his work.

Second—It has aroused a strong *esprit du corps* among our young people. They are drawn together in Christian sympathy.

Third—It has strengthened the bond between the young and the church.

Fourth—It has developed an astonishing fertility in many a life that was only too barren before.

Fifth—Through its instrumentality, largely, over forty earnest workers have been added to the church.

And so we all say, "God bless the Society with the magic name, Y. P. S. C. E.—[Rev. S. Winchester Adriance, Pastor Cong. Church.

From Boscobel, Wisconsin.

This movement brought together a few, honest, warm-hearted Sunday School scholars and younger teachers, and united them in a common aim. I got a hearing with them which I could have secured in no other way. In a town where the influence over the young was to make religion seem of very little account, I was able to make religion seem to be the grand and glorious thing among at least a few people.

Estimating the results, as they always should be estimated, relatively, according to the obstacles to be overcome, I regard the work done through the Society of Christian Endeavor in Boscobel as *very important.*—[Rev. E. S. Morse, formerly Pastor Cong. Church.

From Brandon, Vermont.

I am more and more convinced that this order of organizations is to be fruitful of good,—great good,—the conversion of thousands, and the training of laborers of which the church and Christ have such great need to-day.

The agent of the Y. M. C. A. of Vermont called a few weeks ago, and here for the first time heard of these Societies ; he was much interested, and said "this is just the right movement to answer the question 'What shall be done in places where no Y. M. C. A. can be supported ?'"—[Rev. Walter Rice.

From Washington Heights, Illinois.

Our Committees have been very active and efficient. Absent members have each a resident correspondent, and we have every reason to believe they are still earnest in their Christian endeavor.

At a recent meeting we voted to purchase a wall leaflet of daily reading for each member present and absent, that we may be united in our daily selections of scripture ; also, to take a collection at each "experience meeting" (in small envelopes)—the funds to be devoted to charities of some kind.

Sick members are visited, and flowers sent them at intervals when convalescing. We have every reason to rejoice in the founding of the Society.—[Edward G. Howe, Cong'l Church.

From Limington, Maine.

Our Society started with thirty members, and has steadily progressed in numbers and interest. We think it has been a means of great good among our young people.—[Rev. E. T. Pitts, Pastor Cong'l Church.

From Beloit, Wisconsin.

We find that the Constitution which we have adopted binds us together, and keeps everything in perfect system.

Most of our active members are *active* and ready, each in his own way, which God has appointed, to do what he can. Many of the associate members have become active, and new names are being handed in almost every Sabbath. Our monthly experience meetings are always largely attended, and many new resolutions are formed for the new month, while the experience which each one gives seems to give aid to the other members.

This is a college town, and there are more than two hundred students, many of whom are members of this Society. The relation of the church to our Society is one of warmest affection. Our pastor, Dr. Bushnell, takes the greatest interest in everything we do.

I think many young persons have been led to think more of spiritual things, and seek rest in Him who is ever ready to receive.—[James R. Robertson, Sec. of the Society connected with the First Cong'l Church.

From Palmyra, N. Y.

Our first experience meeting will be long remembered by those who attended ; many thought it was the best meeting ever held in our lecture room. A number spoke of God's love for them, and of their love for Him, whose voices had never been heard, or at least not for a long period, in a public assemblage. God's spirit was surely with us that evening, and we all felt wonderfully blest. So has the Society proved a great blessing to the church, as many have become active members, and thus members of the church, who first joined this Society as associate members.—[Geo. S. Johnson, Pres. of the Society connected with the Presb. Church.

From Newburyport, Mass.

Not a single incident has occurred, nor has any outgrowth been observed which would in any way discredit the wisdom of the formation of such a Society. On the other hand, it has proved its right to be by affording a means of developing young church members in Christian life and endeavor, by creating a mutual interest among its young people, by increasing the attendance and life of all the services of the church, and by serving to bring the pastor and his wife into continual, intimate and delightful connection with the young. We rejoice in the fact that some who are about to enter into the church were led to Christ through the instrumentality of this Society.

Speaking from the standpoint of a pastor, past experience has developed nothing to discourage effort in the line of such a Society. The present is full of achievement, and the future looks big with hope.—[Rev. Charles P. Mills, Pastor of the North Church.

From Chester, N. J.

Our Society has raised during the year one hundred and four dollars and ninety-nine cents ($104,99). The Society has recently completely renovated the parsonage parlor; have made a substantial addition to the library of one of our self-sacrificing missionaries in the Indian Territory, and have taken a share and a half toward the support of the Missionary Ship "Morning Star" in the Pacific Ocean.—[Secretary of the Society connected with the Congregational Church.

From Portland, Maine.

One of the most interesting facts connected with the work of this Society is, that many of the young men in the Sunday School, from 16 to 20 years of age, have been led to Christ and are leading an active and earnest Christian life. The experience meeting has proved a means for young Christians who are usually silent, to make a public confession. There can be no doubt that the Society has been an instrument in God's hand to bless the church, by adding new and earnest life to its ranks; the Sunday School, by giving young and energetic teachers, and to the young, by lifting them from the vanities of the world and giving them a hope that maketh not ashamed.— [Secretary of the Society connected with the St. Lawrence Street Society.

From Boston, Mass.

For a Society less than three months old ours has been a great success.

The attendance at the Young People's Meeting has nearly or quite trebled, and the committees have already done good work. Several members will soon join the church.—[A. J. Abbe, Sec. Young People's Society of Christian Endeavor, Immanuel Church.

From Burlington, Vermont.

The Society of Christian Endeavor of our church has been fruitful of great good. A steady interest is manifested by nearly all the members, and the meetings are well sustained and of exceptional interest. We do not see that any of the troubles and difficulties so often prophesied for these Societies are at all likely to befall us, but we believe we shall grow in numbers, strength and usefulness.

In the revival that took place in our church in connection with the week of prayer, the good work of the Society was plainly manifest, and nearly thirty young people joined the church as the result—From the Society connected with the Winooski Ave. Cong. Church.

From Rochester, N. Y.

By nearly all the active members the obligations have been well kept. The young men have done their part by witness-bearing, prayer and exhortation. Many of the young ladies are in the habit of giving testimony, but more recite passages of Scripture or read a brief, appropriate selection. Our monthly consecration meetings are especially profitable and enjoyable. We regret that we cannot report more conversions, but we are greatly encouraged at what God has done for us, for the following reasons :

1st. All through summer vacations and winter gayeties, when numbers have heretofore decreased and interest flagged, our weekly meetings have been well attended and characterized by an unprecedented degree of activity and fervor.

2d. Much latent talent has been discovered and developed. Little by little the timid ones have been drawn out, and to-day we are getting the best testimony from those whose mouths seemed the most tightly sealed.

3d. All have something to do, and so feel a deeper personal interest in the success of our meetings. One year ago, the time was generally taken up by eight or ten—week after week the same ones—but now it is no uncommon thing for seventy-five to take active part. We recognize the necessity of using the greatest care in the choice of *active* members. All applications for membership are acted upon by the Lookout Committee.

At first many objected to pledging themselves in any way, urging that it was unreasonable and unwise, that such service, to be acceptable, should be voluntary. Many of us, however, have found that that which was once done merely from a sense of duty, soon became a service of love, and all now concede the wisdom of this feature.

A careful record is kept by the Secretary of the attendance and the number who take part in every meeting. At the close of our monthly consecration meeting the roll is called and absentees are reported to the Lookout Committee. Our largest attendance at any one meeting was 147, of which number 72 took part.

The following Committees have been only quite recently added, viz : Sunday School, Visiting, Missionary and Social. All are doing effective service excepting the Visiting Committee, who have not found much in their particular line to do. The Missionary Committee provide for the quarterly Missionary Meetings, which give promise of great interest and usefulness. They have also secured monthly pledges, varying from five cents to one dollar per month, aggregating four hundred dollars per annum. With this we hope to do some good on both home and foreign fields.

Thus we are well organized and equipped for God's service. Our chief danger now is that we may rely too much upon the organization and too little upon the Holy Spirit.—[W. E. Sloan, Cor. Sec. Central Presb. Church, Theo. W. Hopkins, Pastor.

The Question Box.

In response to the invitation to present questions on any point in the work on which information might be wanted, about thirty questions were handed in. They were read at the evening session by Rev. F E. Clark, who called on various persons to answer them. But few of them can be given, and the gist only of the answers.

Ques. Is it best to take a vacation in the summer?

Answered by Granville Staples, of Portland: Yes, for our city Societies at least. So many of our people go away during the months of July and August that I think it better to put all our force into the regular prayer meetings during those months. Then we are fresh for work in the Society by the first of September.

Ques. Will not having topics hinder some from taking part in meeting, as they may not care to speak on that subject?

Answered by Mr. Sewall, of Lowell, Mass.: No, I think not. We cannot know too much about what is going to be done, and we should know it long enough to be able to prepare for it.

Ques. What shall be done with members who fail to take any part in prayer meetings?

Answer. Put them at work somewhere. Use personal effort to get them to do their part both in the meeting and out.

Ques. Would you have all the members lead the meetings in their turn, ladies as well as gentlemen?

Answered by Mr. Page, of Bucksport: It is our custom to have the gentlemen take turns in leading the meetings. In small Societies I think it would be desirable to have the ladies take their turn in leading.

Ques. What shall be done with active members who will not take part in the meetings, or who refuse to obey the rules, or who behave improperly in meeting?

Answered by Mr. Hall, of Lowell: Let them be visited by the Prayer Meeting Committee. If this has no effect, by the pastor. If this fails, let them be expelled.

Ques. Is it best to call the roll of members at the experience meeting, in order that all may have an opportunity of taking part?

Answered by W. H. Pennell, of Portland: We have found in our Society that all do not get a chance, as some are likely to talk too long, unless the roll is called, when all know they are limited in time.

Ques. Will it be wise for Societies to defray the expenses of their delegates to the Annual Conferences ?

Answered by F. B. Knapp : For some reasons it would—otherwise some of those who would best represent us might be unable to attend.

Ques. Is it best to hold our sociables in the church parlors or at private houses ?

Answered by C. H. Hight : In the church parlors. The Society is as much a part of the church as is the Sabbath School, and should be so treated.

Ques. What shall be the method of raising money for necessary expenses of the Society ?

Answered by W. J. Van Patten, Burlington, Vt.: Our Society has no expenses to pay, as the church pays all expenses. I think the expenses should be kept very small, and the church should bear them. Money for special purposes might be raised by giving entertainments, or by subscription, but never by assessment.

Ques. How can the Sabbath School teachers be made recruiting officers for the Young People's Societies ?

Answered by R. T. G. Brown, of Lowell : This must be determined largely by the character of the class, and the teacher's relation to it. The teacher should always be in sympathy with his class. Invite them to the sociables, and then, after they have had a good time, ask them if they do not desire to become members. If the teacher has a special, personal influence over his scholars, let him see if a few timely words will not induce them to join as associate members, and thus they may be led finally to the full enjoyment of all duties and benefits of active membership.

Ques. How much shall the pastor do in the prayer meetings ?

Answered by Rev. G. B. Wing : Very little. He should be felt rather than heard much. The young people's meeting is not the place for a sermon or a lecture from the pastor. He should be like the look-out on board ship, having little to say unless he sees breakers dead ahead, or upon the right or left.

www.ingramcontent.com/pod-product-compliance
Lightning Source LLC
Chambersburg PA
CBHW020527030426
42337CB00011B/565